UNWRITTEN RULES

A short stage play that examines morals and ethics in today's society.

Written by Lesley Fletcher

Unwritten Rules

For any inquiries please contact:

Lesley Fletcher at Lesley@lesleyfletcher.com

Praise

Intense personalities, moral issues, it's dark, it's funny, it twists, it turns ... Unwritten Rules reads like a film!

- Cat Forsley

(catforsley.me – musician, model, actor)

Wonderful dialog style that reads very believable. Lesley has produced a genuine story of deep tooted problems in our world with touch of humor and irony.

- Toni Taylor

(radio host)

UNWRITTEN RULE

CHARACTERS

TARA – 14 year old, jeans-clad, attitude, witty, together, intelligent.

JULIA – Tara's mother, 38 year old, divorced, mother with custody of Tara, yoga master, in control.

RACHEAL – 14 year old friend and neighbour of Tara – jeans-clad, typical, a bit messy, not too much attitude, quieter than most of her friends at school.

DEBBIE – Racheal's mother, widowed, 42 year old alcoholic, frail, ineffective, disheveled.

ANDREA – Julia's younger sister, 32 year old, single, gay, legal assistant.

MOM – Julia and Andrea's mother; Tara's grandmother, young 63 year old, busy, social, loves to talk.

THE SOCIAL WORKER – typical, early 30's rushing, bureaucratic (Stella Wiseman).

SYNOPSIS: A mother experiencing behavioural / emotional difficulties with her teenage daughter conjures a plan to save her daughter at the cost of another life. The story demonstrates classic similarities between generations, while providing humour and realism against a backdrop of deceit and moral deviance.

ACT 1

SCENE 1

The scene opens with Tara bounding into her home after school. Tara's mother is in a lotus position facing the lit fireplace with her eyes shut, deep in concentration. Waterfall music plays throughout the speaker system within the home. Tara enters with a bang, throwing down her knapsack and calls out for her mother without bothering to notice her mother in the living room to her right as she races straight ahead to the kitchen.

Tara: Hey Ma. Wadda-ya doin'? *calling out in a loud voice.*

When there is no answer she pops her head into the living room. Her mother does not respond. Tara performs an eye roll and a headshake.

Tara: Well okay, well since you're not answering I guess I'll just have to tell you...

Tara glances again to see an unmoved figure.

She sighs and throws her arms up, letting them fall to her thighs with a slap.

Tara: You know Ma - stats show that a child who is virtually ignored by her mother seeks love elsewhere – mostly in dark and dirty alleys with drug addicts and **pedophiles**...

Tara pours and drinks a glass of juice leaving fridge door open, empty glass and juice container on the counter while she opens and closes the same 3 cupboards 2-3 times. Each time slamming it louder than the last.

Tara: There's **nothin'** to eat! God. There's only **rabbit** food – do you even **go** grocery shopping?

Pause

Tara: That was a **question.**

(eye roll)

Tara: Ya know – I'd like to know one other kid who comes home to a freakin' zulu-zombie-zen-head who listens to water falls all freakin' day! – Racheal's Mom – you know Racheal? Across the street- my best friend? Well she's got it made. **Her** Mom listens to hip-hop – they dance together every day– they in-ter-act and I gotta come home to this crap.

Voice trails off at the end as she stuffs strawberries in her mouth. Tara's cell phone rings. Tara pulls her i-Phone from her back pocket, taking a quick glance at the screen before answering with her mouth still full.

Tara: Talk to me Racheal *(mumbling, her mouth full of strawberries)*

Pause

Tara: No she can't come over, she's **me-de-ta-ting**.

Pause

Tara: **What**? OhMyGod OhMyGod – I'm comin', I'm comin' – stay on the phone!

Tara runs down the hallway leaving the fridge and cupboards open, glances with hesitation at her still, unmoved mother and runs out the door and across the street where Racheal's mother is being taken away in a body bag.

Tara: *(eyes wide, breathing heavily)* What happened? Did it happen while you guys were dancing?

Racheal : I never told anyone. I never told anyone.

Tara: Told anyone what? Tell me. Tell me!

Tara puts her arm around Racheal's shoulder and together they move quickly away from the ambulance to sit, huddled closely on the front step of Racheal's house. They watch it pull away.

Racheal : I'm sorry I didn't tell you.

Tara: Tell me what? I don't understand!

Racheal is crying.

Racheal: I kinda lied. My Mom was drunk every day when I got home. She would be dancing like an idiot. She **forced** me to dance with her – drinkin' from her bottle of peace – that what she called it. Her bottle of peace... her peace pills and her bottle of peace to wash 'em down... I'm sorry I never told you.

Racheal is crying to the point of sobbing now. Tara stares into the distance and hugs her friend tighter, rubbing her back.

Tara: It's okay...

Pause, quiet voices follow

Racheal: Ever since my Dad died she died too. I tried - (*tearfully*)

Tara: Believe me there is nothing you could've done.

Racheal: I could have told someone – at least.

Tara: What could anyone do? My mom has been dead for years. Ever since my Dad left with his boys. I should have gone with him.

Racheal: Tahhhrah! I can't believe you just said that. Your mother is alive! Mine's dead.

Tara: I'm sorry , I'm sorry – I'm really sorry. That was a really stupid thing to say. I just wanted you to know that I know how you feel. I can't imagine how you feel... I'm so sorry. (*Tara is crying now*)

(*whining*) (*hysteria is creeping into her voice*)

Racheal: What am I gonna do? Where am I gonna live? I don't even know where my brother is. He could be dead too!

Pause

Tara: What about your grandparents?

Racheal: I can't stay with **any** of my Dad's side of the family. Ever since the accident they are so mean to us.

Tara: Why? It was an accident. They should still love you.

Racheal: Well they don't. They blame my mother.

Tara: How 'bout your uncle? I know you hate your cousins but -

Racheal: Tara. He's a perv! I already told you that. **Oh my God! What am I gonna do?** The social worker's gonna come back any minute. What'll they do to me?

Pause – both girls have their elbows on their knees and hands holding their chins.

Tara: You can live with us. Don't worry. Everything will be fine. Don't worry. You can live with us. My Mom'll talk to the social worker. Don't worry.

Racheal takes a deep breath, sighing.

Racheal: Are you sure? Will your Mom say okay?

Tara: Yeah she will and she'll talk to the social people. She'll figure it out. She likes you. Now, don't worry please, please. I'm your best friend. I'll take care of you.

Pause

Rachael: Your mother is perfect.

Tara: Hardly. She smokes pot ya know. She is not perfect like you think she is. She's a freaken space cadet.

Rachael: *(smiling slightly)* But what does she use to cool the munchies? She's a health food freak.

Tara: *(smiling)* Ha! A bag of carrots – we go through a **lot** of carrots.

They both giggle.

Long pause

Rachael: I found her in the bathtub when I came home at lunch. It looked like she was sleeping. She looked so peaceful. But she wouldn't wake up.

Tara: I don't know what to say. It must have been so awful. I can't even imagine losing my mom. She's all I've got.

Rachael: Me too. But you know if your mom says yes, I won't be any trouble. Then we'll have each other.

Tara: Yeah, plus my grandma and my aunt. It'll be fun to have you as my sister. We won't fight like my mom and Andrea do though...

Racheal: No! We'll just be there for each other and have fun.

Tara : Remember when we smoked?

Racheal: Yeah

Tara: Then we bought that huge cookie-dough ice cream but then we had no spoons?

Racheal: Yeah

Tara: We ate it with our fingers. Those were the good ole days.

Racheal: Yeah, I miss summer already. I can't believe my mom's gone, Tara.

Tara: I can't believe it either.

Racheal and Tara face each other holding hands and looking at each other's eyes.

Racheal: I can cook you know. I do it every day anyway.

Tara: I can grocery shop, so you can cook. We can shop together - with a list.

They smile slightly.

Racheal: I'll clean our room. I can stay in your room right? I don't want to be alone.

Tara nods reassuringly.

Tara: I'll do our laundry.

Racheal: I'm never getting married.

Tara: Me either – look what happens.

Racheal: Let's promise right now to always be together.

They pinkie swear by joining each other's pinkie fingers together.

Tara catches Racheal's eye with a bit of a wink.

The girls smile weakly, wiping their tears at the same time.

ACT II

SCENE 1

Earlier that day. It is morning, ambient music is piped through the house. Julia is alone in her modern kitchen, tidying up, washing dishes, dressed for the day in yoga pants, t-shirt with her hair tied in a ponytail, when the home phone rings. Julia takes time to dry her hands and fold the towel before answering. It is Julia's mother – Julia engages in a conversation. We don't hear the caller.

Julia: Hi Ma. What's up?

pause

Julia: Okay, okay sorry.... How are you Mom?

pause

Julia: No. Tara's at school. Why?

Pause

Julia: I can't believe Andrea told you. I asked her not to. Tara **was** suspended. Everything is fine now.

Pause

She replies in a clipped tone.

Julia: This is why... I just told you everything is **fine** I'm handling it. Let's leave it at that.

Pause

Julia: You took the oregano I left for Andrea? Why would you **do** that?

Pause

Julia: It **is** oregano. I grew it in my garden!

Pause

Julia: Big Daddies!

Julia is cracking up, holding her stomach, not making any sound. Long pause as she listens. Julia sends a text from her cell phone while speaking on her home phone.

Julia: Yeah – *(with a laughing sigh)*

pause

Julia: Don't worry. I'll take care of it.

Still laughing lightly.

Julia: Of course I won't tell her! It's **not** Andrea you're talking to.

Julia's i-Phone rings. She glances at the screen.

Julia: Listen, Ma I gotta go. Andrea's calling my cell.

Julia: Love you too, Mom. Bye.

Julia answers her cell phone.

Julia: Hi, Andrea. You just saved me from Mom.

Pause

Julia: I'll tell you when you get here. The front door's open.

Julia hangs up and busies herself tidying the kitchen for a minute before her sister, Andrea arrives.

Andrea: What was so important that we had to talk in person. You know I had to call in late for work. It better be important...

Julia: Just sit down and relax geesh. I made carrot cake and coffee for you. It's important. Trust me. But first we gotta talk about Mom.

Andrea is pacing back and forth.

Andrea: What now?

Julia: You're so clippy today. Lighten up – you never even take a vacation. An hour or two won't kill you.

Andrea silently pours two coffees and cuts some cake making noise with each movement.

Julia: You were right Mom stole the bag of pot from your place. You didn't lose it. She knew it was pot. Told me she never fell for the oregano bullshit. Then she goes on and on about how she wasn't born yesterday and bla bla bla bla.

Andrea: What? She smokes pot? She stole it on purpose? I can't believe it.

Julia: I know, I know. She told me not to tell you though so don't say anything and I'll work it out so she pays me for it – then I'll get you some more.

Andrea: Whatever... but she smoked all that? Impossible. I can't get my head around this at all.

Julia: Oh grow up Andrea! I'm telling you she knew exactly what it was and she took it. You know why? Get this. Cus she wanted to roll big daddies and sell them to the ladies in her bridge club. Her words, I swear. Then after they all smoked she served make-em-yourself ice cream sundaes.

Andrea, visibly relaxing and laughing now, along with Julia.

Andrea: I still can't believe how low they go, just to snag the hostess with the mostess award. Those women are relentless. I'd love to see that bitch Frieda's face!

Julia: Apparently, Frieda was the only one who refused the joint. Guess Mom's going to break Frieda's winning streak. She was in a real snit, Mom said.

Andrea: Ahh well. Good for Mom. *(laughing)*

Julia: Now to business. I really wanted to thank you again for getting your boss to draw up the papers. I really appreciate it you know.

Andrea: I'm still not completely comfortable with the whole thing Julia. It felt wrong. He asked a lot of questions.

Julia pushes the chair violently away from the table.

Julia: Well it's **not** wrong. We've been through this already. Debbie's a drunk. She killed her husband for God's sake! She may as well have put a bullet in him. Racheal needs a chance in life and I can give it to her. What don't you get?

Andrea: Last I heard it was ruled an accident. Who are you to judge her? You're no Mother Theresa. You want Racheal because you think she'll get Tara out of her funk. I'm not stupid, you know. Don't forget, I know all about the trouble you've had with Tara lately. Is she still seeing the psychologist?

Julia: Yeah yeah she is... which reminds me. Why did you tell Mom about her getting suspended? You better not have told her the other stuff because I told you not to. Now every time she phones she's busting my chops about Tara. You're always so holier than thou. You know as well as I do Racheal needs a stable home environment and not only that but Debbie needs time to get her act together. It would only be temporary. I'm actually doing both of them a favour.

Andrea: First of all no, I didn't tell Mom everything. She was all suspicious about something Tara said and I had to give her something. You know what's she's like. And secondly, if you let me finish what I was saying. If you say it's a favour you're lying even to yourself. If it's a favour then, why were you so intent on having legal papers drawn up. It could have been just a verbal agreement with Debbie.

Julia: Well, Debbie's husband's family could go all cuckoo and start trouble. The papers are to cover Debbie's ass.

Andrea: Not to mention your own.

Julia: Look, once and for all – let's get this straight. I am helping Debbie and Tara er.. I mean Debbie and Racheal.

Andrea: So why am I here? I've heard all this already. Now you know how I feel about it. See? You just made a Freudian slip – you said Debbie and Tara.

Julia: Never mind all this bickering.. I just need you to do one more thing. Remember Mom's written rules? We vowed to always take care of our own.

Andrea: We signed that stupid thing when I was ten! You've used it ever since... Just what is it now?

Julia: Well ummm, I was wondering if you wouldn't mind finding someone to witness the signatures. I'm going to get Debbie to sign today. I'm sure you can find someone at work. I really need you for this.

Andrea: I can't find someone so fast!

Julia: No no – no rush. I'll sign and get Debbie to sign. I just need someone to witness them. I'll fill in the dates later.

Andrea: What the hell are you saying? Now you're really pissing me off. Do you realise how illegal this is? Not to mention immoral, unethical?

Julia: There you go again throwing your education around. So I don't work in some fancy schmancy law firm. Just a lowly yoga instructor. That's me -

Andrea: Okay enough! You always pull the same shit on me. I told you before, I'm not going to apologise for who or what I am.

Julia: Will you do it though? You do owe me one or two you know.

Andrea takes a moment to answer, letting out a long drawn breath.

Andrea: Okay I'll do it but after this we're even. Got that? I feel like my own sister is blackmailing me.

Julia: I promise. This is the last favour. I really appreciate it Andrea. No matter what you think. It's so important to me. You're important to me too.

Julia pulls back and holds her sister's face gently with hands cupped on each side.

Julia: Thank you Andrea. I knew I could count on you.

Andrea pulls away.

Andrea: I'd better get going.

Julia: Thanks again. I'll call you later.

Andrea: Yeah yeah ... what about the unwritten rule? (*Andrea's voice fades off as Julia hums loudly. Andrea rushes out the door*)

SCENE 2

Julia hurries to pull out the papers from her desk drawer tucking them into the corner of the kitchen counter. She rushes to put a pen beside it – She pulls out two bottles of liquor, re-setting the automatic coffee maker just as the doorbell rings.

Julia runs to the door hugging her guest (Debbie) as she ushers her in.

Julia: Debbie you poor dear – look at you! How are you?

Debbie, still in her pyjamas, her mascara smudged, is obviously drunk.; her speech is loud and slurred.

Debbie: Oh Julia. You're my best friend ever. What would I do without you. Things got worse. They got worse. Way worse.

Julia: Come on in and sit down. You look like you could use a good strong coffee and a lot of TLC. I'll make us Spanish coffees while you tell me all about it. You know there's nothing we can't handle together. I'm here for you.

Julia busies herself making the coffees while Debbie talks. Julia is sure to put a good dose from each of the bottles of liquor, leaving her own coffee without additions.

Debbie: I just got off the phone with the social worker. She told me they're planning to charge me with manslaughter. I'm going to jail. I'm gonna have to go to jail! They're gonna take Racheal. Just like what happened to me. They put my mother in prison too.

Julia: Okay slow down. What are you talking about? You never told me they took you away from your mother. That's horrible.

Debbie: Yeah like mother like daughter. My mother died in prison. I'm gonna die. I'm gonna die just like my mother. I was in foster homes. I lost my sister. Oh my God. How can this be happening? I swear I thought I was pressing the brake. I didn't mean to kill Johnny. Now the private investigators talked to people. Johnny's family hired them. They want me in jail. They want Racheal in foster care. They won't even take care of their own blood. Say she's tainted. How could my baby be tainted?

Julia: Oh Lord Debbie, how could they be so callous. Racheal is such a beautiful child. Of course it was an accident. Everyone knows that. Let's think things through.

Debbie: I just don't know what to do.

Debbie finishes her coffee in one gulp as Julia races for the bottles and coffee pot.

Julia: What did the social worker say exactly? Did you call your lawyer?

Debbie: I called him but he wasn't there. So typical. They're like oh don't worry we'll have so-and-so take care of it. He's up to date on the case. I'm like; fuck you and I hung up.

Julia: Wow. Anything for extra billings. You know you're going to get charged for the meetings to bring the new one in. Lawyers are leeches taking advantage of people like that. Now what did the social worker say this morning – are you sure you got it right? Tell me exactly what she said.

Debbie: She's like; Debbie, I just wanted to prepare you, they're going to be charging you with manslaughter. Then I said -but, then she cut me off. She says the findings of the private investigator have been filed and have provided enough evidence to bring new charges. Then she says, it's going to be fast so we have to talk about Rachael. And then like the in-laws have refused to talk to her.

Julia: What? She's way out of line. What's she doing calling the in-laws behind your back.

Debbie: I didn't even think of that. She's supposed to be on my side! She's **my** social worker.

Julia: They're all the same. I think they actually live for things to go wrong. What else did the social worker say?

Debbie: Can't trust no one. Not even your own lawyer. Not even your own social worker. She wants to get things rolling she said, to place Rachael, as if she was doing me a favour.

Julia: This is just craziness. I am sure it will get sorted out somehow. **You are not a killer for God's sake. You just made a mistake!**

Debbie: What would I do without you? You're the only one who believes me. The only one in the neighbourhood who even talks to me. I am tainted too. I hate them all. And my doctor – you know what; I fuckin hate that doctor. He won't give me my prescriptions.

Julia: Well that's just not fair. What were you taking? Obviously you need your prescriptions – now more than ever.

Debbie: Well he said no. I begged him. I told him how anxious and depressed I am and he told me I had to stop drinkin and I told him I did and he didn't believe me.

Julia: Listen. Doctors have no compassion anymore. They are all out to cover their own asses. They don't care about humans. Bet you had to pass your card to hear that shit right?

Debbie: Oh yeah – he took my money but wouldn't help me at all. He's like – see about going for counselling and get sober. What a jerk! Let him live a while in my shoes and see the meds fly. Jerk.

Julia: But what were you taking?

Debbie: Only Prozac and Ativan. You'd think I'd asked for heroin or something.

Julia gets up and goes to a cupboard in her kitchen. She pulls out two pill bottles and fishes in a drawer for two plastic baggies.

Julia: Well, this is one thing I can do something about, right now. The cruelty of society is almost too much to bear these days.

She sits at the table and empties the pills from each container in a separate baggie setting them beside Debbie after removing one of each which she also places beside Debbie. Debbie swallows the pills immediately, with a big sigh.

Julia: When I was going through hard times these saved my life. You can have them all and I have more when those are done. I don't need them anymore. Are you sleeping okay?

Debbie: Hell no... The pharmacy cut me off my Ambian. Said I had all my refills. Such bullshit. Then my doctor got involved and said his prescription was for six months. The idiot pharmacy told him all the repeats were dispensed. They're such liars! Oh you're the best friend ever. What can I do to help you. Nothing. (*crying while wiping her tears and nose on her sleeve*). I'm so useless.

Julia: You don't need to do anything. I want to help. That's all. Now enough of this talk. Let's try to make a plan. We need a backup plan – just in case – well, not that it will happen but just in case this asinine idea to throw you in prison for something you didn't do actually happens. Though I just can't imagine...

Both Julia and Debbie are shaking their head.

Debbie: Prison. I'm going to die in prison, just like my poor mother.

Julia appears to be thinking while Debbie continues to drink and wipe her nose.

Julia: I have some sleeping pills but they probably expired. Let me check.

Debbie: I knew you would help me figure something out. You're the best. Gimme expired ones. They'll be fine. Um that is if you don't need them. I am such a loser. I can pay you for them. How much would they be? I am taking my best friend's pills. How terrible!

Julia refills Debbie's coffee and re-pours the liquor liberally into the large cup.

Julia: Don't say that Debbie! This is temporary. Look you can have them. Just don't get them mixed with the others. I don't want you to be sleeping all day and awake all night.

Debbie: Ha! You're too much. Taking care of me like this. Nobody else cares – nobody. *(sniffling)*

Julia: Well I certainly do! You remember what we talked about last week. About the papers?

Debbie: A little...

Julia: I had the papers drawn up so that I would be Racheal's legal guardian. But of course it's only temporary.

Debbie: You did that for me? Wow no one has ever been so nice to me.

Julia: Remember they're just papers and I can tear them up anytime you like. Once they're signed you can send Racheal over anytime that you are ready. I know it's not easy but I feel you need a break. Time to get yourself back to you, you know? You know what they say; time heals all wounds. Now with this stupid thing with the charges, the pressure must be too much to bear having to put a front on for Racheal.

Debbie: Oh you know me so well. Such an angel you are. I need time to get my act together, it's true. Now 'specially with the charges. Poor Rachael having me for a mother.

Julia: Okay, well let me see if I can even find those papers.

Debbie: I'm having such a wonderful time with you. It almost feels like I'm in the hands of an angel. And to think I was ready to kill myself this morning. You saved my life. I'm serious.

Julia gets up, opening the highest cabinet door where her pill bottles are stashed.

Julia: Debbie, don't be talking that way.
Everything is fixable. We just need a plan. Oh, and
here's the sleeping pills. Just taking care of you. I
know you would do the same.

*Julia fills another plastic baggie with pills and hands them
over to Debbie. Debbie puts them with the other two bags
and helps herself to another full mug of only liquor. Julia
tops her own cup with coffee and whipping cream adding
some cream to Debbie's drink. Debbie takes a noisy slurp,
leaving traces of whipping cream on her nose and face.*

Julia: Gotta keep the balance Debbie. All about the
balance. I remember now where I put the papers.
Just a sec.

*Julia heads back behind the kitchen counter letting her eyes
scan the surfaces, opening and closing drawers.*

Debbie: You know who I ran into the other day?
Helene. You know what she said? Such a fuckin'
bitch. I was ready to smash her French face in.

Julia: (*answering from behind the counter*) What did
that two face say to you? Don't tell me she talked
about the accident. She has no couth what-so-ever!

Debbie: No, no it was about you. I'm like – who the hell are you? How do you know that? Who told you that? It's not true! I stuck up for you Julia. You're my friend. I know you're not a whore.

Julia: What? She called me a whore? That cow!

Debbie: Well, she didn't say whore exactly but she was talking about child support and stuff, you know, and then she said she was surprised you still got support from Mike being that Tara wasn't his.

Julia: She was talking about child support? What else did she say?

With the papers in her hand Julia dashes to the kitchen table facing Debbie.

Debbie: She was all bragging that Mike got this huge contract and you wouldn't see a penny more in child support or alimony. I was like, what the fuck, what's she talking about, so then I go over to them all talking... and that's when I told her off.

Julia: Them all? She was talking about Mike's contracts and our settlement? Holy shit. Why didn't you tell me this before. When did this happen? Oh my God – she must be sleeping with Mike. What an idiot he is trusting her. Wow.

Debbie: It only happened yesterday or maybe a couple a days ago, at the mall. I was going to tell you last night but then I didn't. I'm so sorry I didn't call you last night. *(crying)*

Julia: No, no don't cry about this. It's okay, really. Just tell me what happened. I need to know everything.

Debbie: Well when I went over and yelled at her to keep her big fat mouth shut then she pushed me out of the circle and then, don't get mad... I spit on her fancy dodad shoes.

Julia: Why would I get mad at that? *(laughing)* Then what happened?

Debbie: Then she had a hissy fit and went all ballistic. Her face turned purple. She's like – These are Steve Madden! I'm like – I don't care who's mad cus I'm mad. And that's when she lost it cus everybody started laughing at her and then she pulled my hair and that was it. I got super mad and I kicked her ass.

Julia: You beat her up? Oh my God Debbie!

Debbie: No I didn't beat her up. I literally kicked her in the ass when she bent over to get the shoe she threw at me. She had this big foot print mark on her white jeans, then she was like the Tasmanian devil, she was so mad but she still didn't shut up.

Julia: Unbelievable. Wait,wait. Who's everybody?

Debbie: Everybody. You know the women she hangs around with. Then one of them stopped laughing and told me to tell you about the twelve million dollar contract and what Helene was saying about you. And then I said I would.

Julia: Twelve million!

Debbie: Yeah and that Tara wasn't his kid. Then she says it again about your yogi – guru. That it was your guru's kid but no one's supposed to know and that's when I gobbed on her other shoe. And she went all ape-shit again and she was screamin' and causin' a huge commotion. "These are Steve Madden, these are Steve Madden!"

Julia: Then what?

Debbie: Well that's when things go out of hand cus security was coming so I go to take off and POCK, I got a Steve Madden shoe right to my head, behind my ear. Then, get this, security grabs her right? Cus she attacked me. I'm like, I don't need this shit, I'm in enough shit already and I took off fast.

Julia: You did the right thing, taking off but you know what, these are all just vicious rumours. I'm glad you told me but I am not the least bit concerned. How would he ever land a contract like that? Let's not give it another thought. There are so many more important things to do today.

Debbie nods her head, rubbing behind her ear where the shoe had hit her. Julia laid the stack of papers on the table with a pen alongside.

Julia: Look, I found the papers. I already signed them. All you need to is sign them, here, and here on the three copies *(Julia points to the places on the papers)* and I'll only fill in the dates when you're ready for Racheal to come live here for a bit.

Debbie signs the papers without reading anything while Julia turns the pages, pointing out the places to sign.

Debbie: You're really my best friend in the world. Thank you so so much.

Debbie polishes off the rest of her coffee and promptly falls asleep with her head on the kitchen table just as Julia's mother walks into the kitchen.

Mom: I tried calling but you didn't answer ...

Her voice trails off as she glances toward the kitchen table.

Whispering.

Mom: What's she doing here? Isn't she the one that killed her husband?

Julia: Shhhhh! Mom, listen, I may have a problem. You know Marie Claude's daughter Helene?

Mom: Yes, what about her?

Julia: Well, I think she's sleeping with Mike.

Mom: She's married –

Julia: Since when is that a reason not to sleep with someone? Anyway, listen. I don't care who Mike sleeps with but Helene has a big mouth and Mike told her about Tara not being his and now she's spreading it around at the mall. There was a gag order on that and now it's going to cost me big time to get him back to court.

Mom: Do you have money problems dear? Is that why you started dealing drugs?

Julia: Don't be ridiculous! I am NOT a drug dealer!

Mom raises her eyebrows as she points out the stash of prescription drugs on the table. She brings her fingers to her lips to hush Julia while pointing to the passed-out Debbie.

Mom: And all that weed. In my day ... what looks like a duck is likely a duck. Just saying -

Julia: Well, it's not your day and I'm not a drug dealer. I'm just helping Debbie out.

Mom: They said that in my day too. We called it "holding for a friend". Anyway, it's no matter to me. Let's just forget it for now. God knows only too well what I've had to do for the sake of you girls. I'm not here to judge.

Julia rolls her eyes and shakes her head.

Julia: There's more Mom. Mike told Helene who then told everyone who would listen that he got a twelve million dollar contract and I wouldn't see any of it.

Mom: Twelve million? That's some serious change! You know our motto. We take care of our own. Period. No matter what.

Julia: I know. So do you think you can help?

Mom: Give me a day. I drive Marie Claude to the casino twice a month. I'll be talking to her about that daughter of hers.

Julia raises her eyebrows, with her jaw dropped, staring at her mother.

Mom: Don't look at me like that. She pays me twenty bucks and five percent off the top of her winnings. That twenty lasts me the whole time I'm there. Anyway the point is she is stealing from the grandkids' accounts. Her husband put money aside for years for those kids and he'd kill her if he ever found out, even if he is a little demented these days. I'm sure I can get her to put a muzzle on that whore of a daughter of hers and even get her to tell everyone that she made it all up. Leave it to me.

Julia is pacing.

Julia: I'm calling Mike right now! That son-of-bitch.

While Julia is dialing, re-dialing and pacing, Mom snoops around, opening drawers and cupboards nosily. Mom then helps herself to a coffee with a shot and a dollop of cream.

Loud whisper.

Julia: What are you looking for?

Mom: Shhhh! Keep your voice down. You'll wake the dead.

Pointing her thumb to the now stirring Debbie, who lifts her head and promptly bangs it back down on the table. Julia puts her finger to her lips in a hush motion and re-dials the number for the fourth time.

Mom: I'm looking for where you stash your pot. I need some more...

Julia: Oh. My. God.

Julia shakes her finger and waves for quiet as she engages in conversation.

Julia: Hi Mike, how're things?

Pause

Julia: Yeah, well I heard things are going very, very well actually.

pause

I heard that you're sleeping with the village voice. That's what I heard.

pause

No, I don't care who you sleep with.

pause

Oh, you don't know who or what I'm talking about? Maybe your memory will be refreshed in front of the judge?

pause

If I told you I heard twelve million little things would that ring the bells of Mounting Ste. Helene?

Julia directs a silent giggle toward her mother.

You heard me. You think you can hide that shit when she spreads rumours faster than she spreads her legs?

pause

I called to give you the heads up. I'm taking you back to court on two issues. One is the money and the other is the gag order. You better watch your freaken pillow talk in future because you just broke the contract and you know what that means?

pause

No? Well go back and read it, you moron.

pause

You think we can work it out? How's that? The damage is already done.

Julia is beaming at her mother, giving her a thumbs-up.

Let me think about it. A million may seem like a lot but.. but I need time to think about it. It'll be a lot more if we go to court. You know that right?

pause

Okay. Give me a day. I'll get back to you. And see if you can't double that. Ciao.

Julia is dancing the happy dance all around the kitchen. Mom looks on with great pride in her daughter's accomplishment. She rushes over to give her a hug.

Mom: So can this be the end of the drug dealing once and for all. Except of course the odd bag of pot.

Julia throws back her head, laughs and hugs her mother tightly, twirling her in a circle.

Julia: A couple of million should do it. Yes Mom. I promise. No more dealing in prescription drugs from now on. Now let's get that pot for you.

Mom: You know if you give me the name of your supplier, I would be more than happy to go direct.

Julia: No, no. I have no problem getting for you. Trust me, you don't want to know these people. Besides, we can't afford to have him get busted.

Mom: Are you suggesting I may be indiscreet?

Julia: No, not at all (*laughing*). I just want to see you more often!

Julia gives her Mom a bag of weed ushering her out the door. She returns to the kitchen to find Debbie awake and drinking more coffee.

Debbie: Oh sorry. I must've fallen asleep.

Julia: Oh, just for a minute. You must be exhausted. Why don't you head home and have a nice hot relaxing bath, wash your hair and treat yourself to a lovely lunch? Will Racheal be coming home for lunch?

Debbie: Oh yeah, she is. I'm gonna do that. Thank you so, so much for all your help. You're the best.

Julia gathers the pills and left-over bottles and places them in a plastic bag. She helps the stumbling Debbie and gives her a quick hug as she pushes her gently out of the door and hands over the plastic bag.

Julia: Please don't thank me any more Debbie. It's nothing. Really. Now off you go for that bath. We'll talk soon.

As Julia leans to close the door she does a double fisted victory pump followed by giant jumps and rapid hand clapping. She stops, places her hands in a yoga prayer position and takes three deliberate deep breaths, exhaling slowly.

ACT III

SCENE 1

The scene picks up from scene one with Julia in her yoga pose in the living room. The front door has just slammed shut. Julia immediately pops up and runs to peek out of the window of the door. She quickly ducks down with her hand clamped over her mouth, eyes wide. She crawls to retrieve her cell phone from one of the living room chairs speaking to herself as she dials.

Julia: Stay calm, stay calm, stay calm. Answer – answer – answer damn it!

Julia: Andrea. Thank God. Say nothing, just listen carefully. Do as I say. Debbie's dead. I need the papers signed right this minute. You have to come over and bring that signature machine thingy. *Short pause.* I know you can get to it. You have the code.

No, no, no, no, no! Debbie was here already and signed them. I just have to date them. There are three copies. If I don't have those papers signed **everything's going to fall apart.**

Pause as Julia listens and peeks out of the window. She ducks down quickly and continues speaking rapidly.

Julia: The social worker is there now. I'll go delay things. Come in through the back and don't be seen! As soon as it's done – take off fast. We **have** to make this work. I know I can count on you. Oh, and date them for three weeks ago. Text me when you're clear.

Julia stands up once again, running her hands over her hair, pulling down her t-shirt and smoothing her pants. She takes a deep breath and heads out the front door as if in a rush.

She runs to the two girls who are now standing crying and puts her arms around them.

Julia: What happened here? What's going on Tara?

Tara: Mom! Debbie's dead and now they want to take Racheal away.

Julia turns to Racheal.

Julia: Oh honey, I'm so sorry. You poor thing.

Julia pulls both girls closer and whispers.

Julia: I'll take care of everything. Don't worry.

S.W. : My name is Stella Wiseman. Were you a close friend of Debbie?

Julia: Yes, yes. I'm Julia Harrington, Tara's mother. Debbie and I were very close. What happened here?

The social worker indicates she won't speak in front of the girls.

Julia: Why don't you girls go across and sit on our steps Tara? Thanks.

S.W. : Racheal called 911 at 12:30 today. She found her mother in the bathtub, dead.

Julia gasped.

Julia: Oh my Lord, how awful. What a tragedy. Did she drown?

S.W.: We're not sure yet of the cause but I think it was suicide.

Julia gasps again.

Julia: I can't believe this.

S.W.: I'll be taking Racheal into child protection. Since you were a close friend perhaps you can let her know. She may take it better, hearing it from you.

Julia: That won't be necessary. Debbie signed over guardianship to me three weeks ago. We were just delaying it until she and Racheal were ready.

Julia manages to squeeze out a few tears and sniffles while she sneaks a peak at her phone.

S.W. : Debbie never mentioned this to me. I'll have to inspect...er see the paperwork of course. It's all highly irregular... I'm going to have to call this in to my supervisor for advisement.

The social worker walks a few steps away eying Julia suspiciously as she is speaking rapidly on the phone. Julia checks her phone again. She waves to the girls giving them a sign that all was under control.

S.W. : I'll need a copy of that paper work. If everything is order Racheal may stay with you. The department will need to keep a close eye on her with regular follow-ups. Racheal is going to need outside support. I'll be making sure she gets it and report directly to child services. She requires a healthy, stable environment.

The social worker is staring at Julia with squinted eyes. Her arms are folded tightly across her chest.

Julia: Of course she does. You can count on me. I'll be happy to team up for Racheal's sake. I'll run and get the paperwork. Be back in a minute.

The social worker fishes in her bag, extracting a business card. Julia accepts the card and runs across to her home.

SCENE 2

The living room is guest ready with bowls of nuts, cut up vegetables, chips and a bottle of champagne with wine glasses. Julia is humming and smiling as she flits about plumping cushions. Standing back she admires the room. She lights the candles and incense then takes a moment to smell the fresh cut flowers.

Mom and Andrea enter through the front door. Andrea is carrying a heavy bag.

Julia: Hi, happy Friday!

Julia rushes to hug them both. She is beaming with smiles as are her mother and sister.

Mom: Wow, Julia! Look how beautiful everything is.

Andrea scoots to smell the flowers.

Andrea: Time to celebrate! Where are the girls?

(Laughing)

Julia: Oh, they're doing a zombie marathon upstairs. They had me rent seven movies. They're too much! They said they would be down later. To tell the truth I am happy to have some good old adult time.

Mom: Then let's get this party going shall we? I brought the biggies!

Andrea: And I brought the wine.

Julia opens the bottle of champagne, pours three glasses and distributes them.

Julia: Before we get started, I need to make a toast.

Mom has already lit a joint which they pass around. They remain standing.

Julia: A toast to the best mother and sister anyone could ever hope to have. Our family motto of taking care of our own was really put to the test and I am ever so grateful to both of you for all of your help. I love you both so much.

Thanks to our accomplishments I am rich in both money and love. The addition of Racheal to our family really made a difference to Tara's and my emotional state. The two of them are like sisters and I have you guys to thank over and over and over again.

The three of them burst into fits of giggles, clinking glasses at the end of Julia's speech. Julia sits down as the joint continues to be passed and the wine poured from a fresh bottle.

Mom: My damage control intervention worked out pretty good. Now I get thirty bucks from Marie Claude every time I take her to the casino. She was 'shook' as they say now.

Andrea: I'm relieved it all worked out. I was worried about Tara too, you know.

Julia: She's okay now. Her and Racheal go to the same therapist so she thinks she's going to help Racheal. Tara's calmed down a lot. I don't have to do that ignoring thing anymore.

The doorbell rings.

Julia: Holy shit! What day is this? Oh my God it's the social worker! – Mom, say nothing. Pretend you're sleeping. Andrea, mess her hair, cover her with a blanket and hide everything on the table **fast.**

Julia opens the door to the social worker.

S.W.: Hello Julia. I'm here for our appointment ...

The social worker's voice trails off as she glances in the living room. Her eyes dart back and forth. She enters sniffing the air and squints suspiciously at Julia and her sister and mother.

Julia: Yes of course, come in. Stella, this is my sister Andrea and my mother. *Julia lowers her voice to a whisper.* Mom just got back from chemo.

The social worker ignores the introduction.

S.W.: I smell marijuana.

Andrea is smiling.

Andrea: Hello Kitty. *(She makes a cat clawing motion with her right hand)* My mom has a prescription. It's for the nausea.

The social worker pulls at her skirt and blazer, running her hand through her hair. She quickly turns back to Julia.

Julia: Please go through to the kitchen Stella. I'll go upstairs and fetch the girls.

As the social worker heads to the kitchen, Julia mouths to her sister questioningly. "Hello Kitty?" Andrea waves her off, laughing. Julia runs upstairs. Mom is shaking with laughter and peeks out from the blanket. Andrea indicates to her to keep her eyes closed.

Julia runs back into the room wide-eyed with her arms in the air and whispers.

Julia: Holy shit! They're not up there.

The social worker enters from the kitchen with the two girls following her. They are made up as zombies, walking flat footed and shuffling with their arms in front of them. Tara who is following Racheal bumps into her as Racheal stops suddenly. They regain their zombie poses, giggling.

S.W. : I don't know what's going on here but these two were chugging back zombies in the kitchen. There were bottles all over. I have to write this up! These two are coming with me right now. They're going into a temp location for the weekend.

Julia: Please, please don't do this. You must be mistaken, Stella. There is a misunderstanding. That's all.

S.W. : Misunderstanding or not they are coming into my custody. You can plead your case in front of Judge Jones at eight sharp Monday morning. Now good night to you all.

The girls follow the social worker out the door, stumbling and giggling..

Andrea calls out while making the same cat claw motion as before.

Andrea: Bye bye Kitty. Meeeooow! *And promptly bursts into uncontrollable laughter.*

Mom throws off the blanket and joins the laughter.

Julia stands with her hands on her hips.

Julia: What is the matter with you people? How can this seem the least bit funny? She has my babies! Andrea, why on earth did you call her Kitty? What's going on here? They have been taken away and all you two can do is laugh.

Mom: Pipe 'er down Julia. Chill out. They'll be fine.

Andrea: I know her from Pouncers. She's a real piece of work.

Julia sinks heavily into her chair staring back and forth between her mother and her sister who continue to laugh.

Mom: Oh Julia – you look so funny when you're shocked.

Andrea: Mom knows I'm gay Julia. She always has ... you never needed to hold that over me.

Mom: Pouncers, hello kitty, I love it! Did you see her face?

Julia: What the fuck is Pouncers?

Andrea: It's a gay bar in the village. I took Mom once. You should come sometime.

Julia gulps her wine and refills her glass, drinking half a glass more shaking her head.

Julia: What the hell does this have to do with anything?

Mom: Tell her Andrea!

Andrea picks up the wine bottle to use as a microphone and starts dancing seductively, undulating her hips. She sings with a deliberate lisp.

Andrea: Me and Judge Jones ...We gotta be extra careful of who sees us together.

Julia stands suddenly grabbing the bottle roughly from Andrea's hands, throws it back and takes a big gulp, wiping her mouth with the back of her hand. Andrea sinks into her chair. Julia uses the same bottle as her own microphone.

Julia: R.E.S.P.E.C.T. That is what you've earned from me... R.E.S.P.E.C.T.

Andrea and Mom rise and sing together with Julia, dancing and using a thrusting chest and arm movement.

Giggling they collapse into their chairs, light another joint and sigh simultaneously. They clink glasses.

Julia: You guys are the best.

Mom pops up suddenly from her chair, grabbing one of the wine bottles, taking a swig before placing it back on the table. She wipes her mouth with the back of her hand.

Mom: I'll bet I know where Kitty took the girls ... (*singing, complete with the dance moves to the song YMCA*) to the Y.M.C.A.. She took them, yes, to the Y.M.C.A.

Andrea and Julia groan as they get up to join her on several repeats of the YMCA song.

CLOSE CURTAIN – The End

About the Author

Lesley Fletcher is a Montreal artist and a writer,
dividing her time between the two crafts while juggling
the complexities involved with marketing and
promotion for both her books, plays and multiple art
pieces. She freelances daily for content, blog posts and
articles with an emphasis on health, family, mental
health and human interests.

Lesley currently has four books published under Inspiration Import. Her latest release, **5 Pillar of the Gypsy**, a mix of art and poetry/prose has been very well received and continues to be a source of inspiration to both herself and her readers.

She is very excited to be working on her first novel – **Chrystal Ball Persuasion**.

Other Books by this Author

Prom Girls a Rite of Passage

(ages 14+ to seniors)

Review: "Prom Girls is not as light and fluffy as you might expect. I like the funny stories and the sad stories equally. One of the stories is written in the language of 'texting' as a young man describes his anxieties of asking out a girl."

All I Want for Christmas is a Wishmas Tree

(ages 7 – 11)

Review: " I read the Wishmas Tree and I love it! I am so amazed by your writing skills. You really get the target audience and write for that level, it's not easy to switch styles so easily. You must have been a writer in a past life. "

Hey Angel!

(ages 2 – 7 – early reader)

Review: "A beautiful book for your children. Lesley writes in a rhyme style children love and her Angel topic is a good moral lesson for all children to learn. I am old and still believe in my guardian angel's help in getting me through tough times."

5 Pillars of the Gypsy (poetry and art)

Review: "I enjoyed this collection of poetry more than any I have read previously. Some of the poems are musical and had an incantatory effect on me. Lesley has adapted a beautiful style of writing poetry. She uses a bit of the traditional style and a diverse technique of writing. All of the poems are easily interpreted and many are heartwarming. I look forward to reading more poetry written by this very talented author."

Coming in 2016 – Chrystal Ball Persuasion

(a contemporary novel)

Connect with Lesley Fletcher

I really appreciate you taking the time to read my play. If you enjoyed the read please consider leaving a review or email me your comments, if you prefer. Thanks for taking the time to read **Unwritten Rules**.

I would love to connect! Here are my social media coordinates:

Friend me on Facebook:

http://facebook.com/inspirationimport

Follow me on Twitter: http://twitter.com/gypsyles

Subscribe to my blog:

http://inspirationimport.wordpress.com

Subscribe to my blog:

http://journeyofthegypsy.wordpress.com

Connect on LinkedIn:

www.**linkedin**.com/pub/dir/**Lesley/Fletcher**

Visit my website: http://www.lesleyfletcher.com

www.ingramcontent.com/pod-product-compliance
Lightning Source LLC
Chambersburg PA
CBHW060535030426
42337CB00021B/4273